Louis
Moyse
Flute
Collection

Volume II

Johann Sebastian Bach

SONATAS

for Flute and Piano

Realization of the Figured Bass by Louis Moyse

In Two Volumes

G. SCHIRMER, Inc.

DISTRIBUTED BY
HAL•LEONARD®
CORPORATION
7777 W. BLUEMOUND RD. P.O. BOX 13819 MILWAUKEE, WI 53213

PRÉFACE

Les sept sonates pour flûte et piano de J. S. Bach présentées dans ces volumes, ainsi que la suite pour flûte seule, sont parmi les oeuvres les plus connues du répertoire flûtistique.

Cette nouvelle édition comporte les trois sonates pour flûte et piano (la troisième incomplète), la suite en la mineur pour flûte seule, les trois sonates pour flûte et basse chiffrée, ainsi que la sonate en sol mineur (écrite pour le violon mais adoptée par les flûtistes). Les chiffrages des 4ème, 5ème et 6ème sonates ont été relevés d'après l'édition de la Bach-Gesellschaft.

Pour les articulations, j'ai toujours tenu compte le plus possible des indications données par la Bach-Gesellschaft, et de leur signification quant à leur expression du point de vue mélodique ou rythmique. Mais il est certain qu'à l'époque les possibilités techniques de la flûte (et des flûtistes) étaient beaucoup plus limitées que de nos jours, et je n'ai pas hesité à prendre la liberté de faire certains changements lorsqu'ils s'avéraient désirables, ceci dans le but d'utiliser au maximum les ressources actuelles de la flûte.

Quant aux groupes, ornements, petites notes, trilles, etc. il y a bien entendu plusieurs façons de les interpréter ; dans certains cas le doute n'est pas possible, mais pour d'autres, pour lesquels d'autres théories peuvent s'appliquer, j'ai indiqué entre parenthèses différentes possibilités, laissant a l'exécutant la faculté de choisir.

Enfin, en ce qui concerne les nuances, il n'y en a quasi aucun d'indiquées dans la Bach-Gesellschaft, comme c'est généralement le cas pour les oeuvres de cette époque ; celles que j'ai mises sont basées sur mon interpretation personnelle.

L.M.

PREFACE

The seven sonatas for flute and piano and the suite for solo flute by J. S. Bach are among the best-known works of the flutist's repertoire.

This new edition contains, in two volumes, the three sonatas for flute and piano (the third is incomplete), the suite in A minor for flute alone, the three sonatas for flute and figured bass, and the sonata in G minor (written for violin but adopted by flutists). The figured bass of the fourth, fifth and sixth sonatas have been realized according to the figuration given in the Bach-Gesellschaft edition.

The melodic and rhythmic articulation indications follow those of the Bach-Gesellschaft as closely as possible. But in Bach's time the technical possibilities of the flute (and the capabilities of flutists) were certainly much more limited than they are today. Therefore, we have not hesitated to change some of the indications when we felt it was desirable, to make full use of the resources of the modern flute. In doing so we have always been careful to respect the melodic and rhythmical meaning of the phrasing indicated by Bach.

There are, of course, many ways of interpreting ornamentation. In certain cases there is no doubt how to execute them, but in the others for which several variants are possible we have indicated the different possibilities in parentheses, leaving to the player the right to choose the one he prefers.

There are almost no dynamic indications in the Bach-Gesellschaft. Those that appear here are based on my personal interpretation.

L.M.

Sonata IV

Johann Sebastian Bach
(1685 - 1750)
Realization of the figured bass
by Louis Moyse

* All trills should start on the
note above and on the beat.

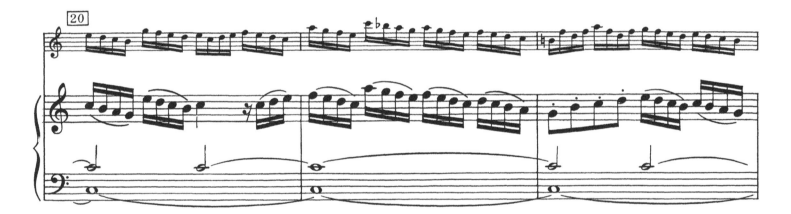

4

Allegro

Menuett I

Menuett II

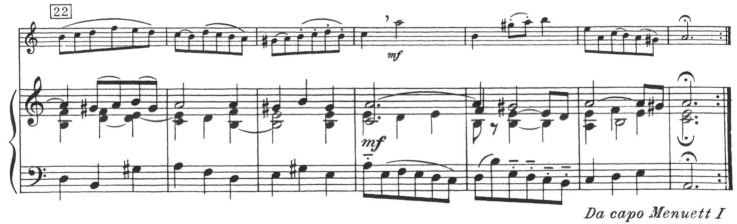

Da capo Menuett I

Sonata V

Realization of the figured bass
by Louis Moyse

Adagio ma non tanto

12

Allegro

*ad libitum

*ad libitum

Andante

Allegro

Flute

Louis Moyse Flute Collection

Volume II

Johann Sebastian Bach

SONATAS

for Flute and Piano

Realization of the Figured Bass by Louis Moyse

In Two Volumes

G. Schirmer, Inc.

DISTRIBUTED BY

HAL•LEONARD®
CORPORATION
7777 W. BLUEMOUND RD. P.O. BOX 13819 MILWAUKEE, WI 53213

Sonata IV

Flute

Johann Sebastian Bach
(1685 - 1750)

*All trills should start on the note above and on the beat.

All dots and dashes written under or at the end of a slur indicate the note should be tongued.

Flute

Adagio

p espressivo

mp   *cresc.*

f   *p*

cresc. molto   *rit.*   *f*

Menuett I

p

mp   *poco cresc.*   *mf*

Menuett II

p dolce

p

cresc.   *mf*

pp   *cresc.*

mf   *Da capo Menuett I*

Sonata V

Adagio ma non tanto

Flute

Allegro

*ad libitum

*ad libitum

Allegro

Flute

Sonata VI

Allegro

Siciliano

Flute

Allegro assai

Sonata VII

Flute

Flute

*ad libitum

Sonata VI

Adagio ma non tanto

Realization of the figured bass
by Louis Moyse

Siciliano

* or

** or

Allegro assai

Sonata VII

Realization of the figured bass
by Louis Moyse

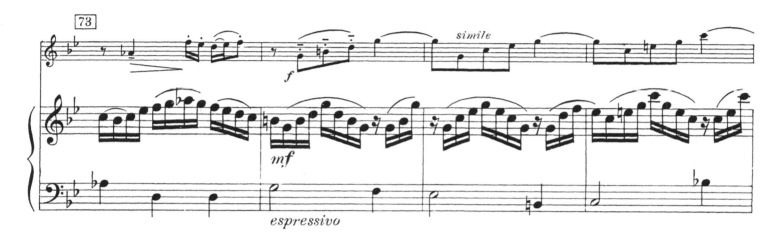

Adagio

Allegro

*ad libitum